Parchment Craft
Embossing Art
Volume 1.

By Lauren Berry

Copyright © 2014 Lauren Berry

All rights reserved.

ISBN: 978-1492152958
ISBN-13: 1492152951

Parchment Craft.
Embossing Art
Volume 1.

First Published in Great Britain 2014 by Purely Parchment Craft, Stoke on Trent

Printed 2014

Text copyright © Lauren Berry

Photographs and design copyright © Lauren Berry 2014

All rights reserved. No part of this book, text, illustrations, templates or photographs may be reproduced or transmitted in any form or by any means of print, photoprint, microfilm, microfiche, photocopier, internet or in any way known or as yet unknown, or stored on a retrieval system, without written permission obtained from Lauren berry.

The author accepts no responsibility for consequences arising from the information, advice or instruction given in this publication.

ISBN: 978-1492152958

ISBN-13: 1492152951

Supplies

If you have any trouble finding supplies and materials that are suggested in this book please refer to the website at:

www.lozzberry.com

Contents

Introduction	6
Tools and Materials	7
Fur and Feathers	10
Red Templates Explained	13
It's All In The Eyes	14
Tips and Tricks	16

Patterns

Eagles	18
Harvest Mice	24
Howling Wolf	28
Macaw	32
Tiger Cub	38
Rock Dragon	44
Pegasus	50
Hummingbird	54
Cat and Mouse	60
Christmas Robins	66

Patterns Included in this Book

EAGLES

HUMMING BIRD

TIGER CUB

HARVEST MICE

MACAW

HOWLING WOLF

CHRISTMAS ROBINS

CAT AND MOUSE

ROCK DRAGON

Introduction

No craft combines style, beauty and elegance quite like parchment craft. The subtle shades and gentle patterns captivate audiences, and the tactile nature of the embossing fills every viewer with the indescribable need to touch and stroke the art. Parchment craft lends itself perfectly to animals; their captivating eyes and beautiful shapes are expressed perfectly through the simple monochromatic tones of the vellum.

You don't need to be a skilled artist to create your own masterpiece. You don't even need to have much experience with parchment craft. This book will guide you through 10 projects, step by step, explaining in detail how to create all of the effects you need to make the image.

For experienced parchment crafters this book is dedicated to the glory of embossing, using the tools to create intricately shaded images with none of the fiddlyness associated with lacework.

So no pricking out - it's all about the texture.

Close Ups

Each project includes detailed images that are just as useful as the written instructions.

These images are particularly important when completing the trickier parts of the project. Study them closely as you complete your parchment craft, and remember to keep turning your work over to see how it is coming along.

Tools and Materials

Parchment crafters can get a bit obsessed with tools. There are nearly a hundred different types and each has its own particular use; some are vital and you will struggle without them, but many are only used sparingly.

This book is dedicated entirely to embossing; using different sized ball tools to deform the vellum; changing it from a semi-translucent grey to purest white. As most parchment craft tools are used for 'pricking out' (poking little holes in the vellum) you will actually need very few tools to complete all the projects in this book. The tools needed for each project are listed at the beginning of each pattern's instructions.

Pergamano vs PCA

It pays to be picky with your equipment and I only use the old-style blue Pergamano tools. There are newer pink/purple ones on the market but I find the blue ones the most comfortable to work with for long periods of time. But that's just me, and you should chose the tools you like best. PCA (Parch Craft Australia) produce superb quality tools in a fetching aluminium finish, and they are easily of the same quality as Pergamano.

But you don't have to use brands. Many small-scale hobby shops sell their own parchment craft tools which are perfectly suitable. Try all the tools you can before you buy – not just the first you see - this way you maximise the chances of buying the best ones for you. Parchment craft tools are not cheap, but they last for a lifetime if you treat them with some respect. Keep your tools clean, dry and in a protective case, such as a pencil tin.

Below is a list of all the tools you will need to complete every single project in this book.

Parchment Craft Vellum

This is the most important piece of equipment, in fact parchment craft is impossible without it. Vellum is a special type of plasticised paper that is thicker and silkier to touch than normal paper. When pressed the vellum does not tear like standard paper, instead it stretches and deforms, changing to white as it does so.

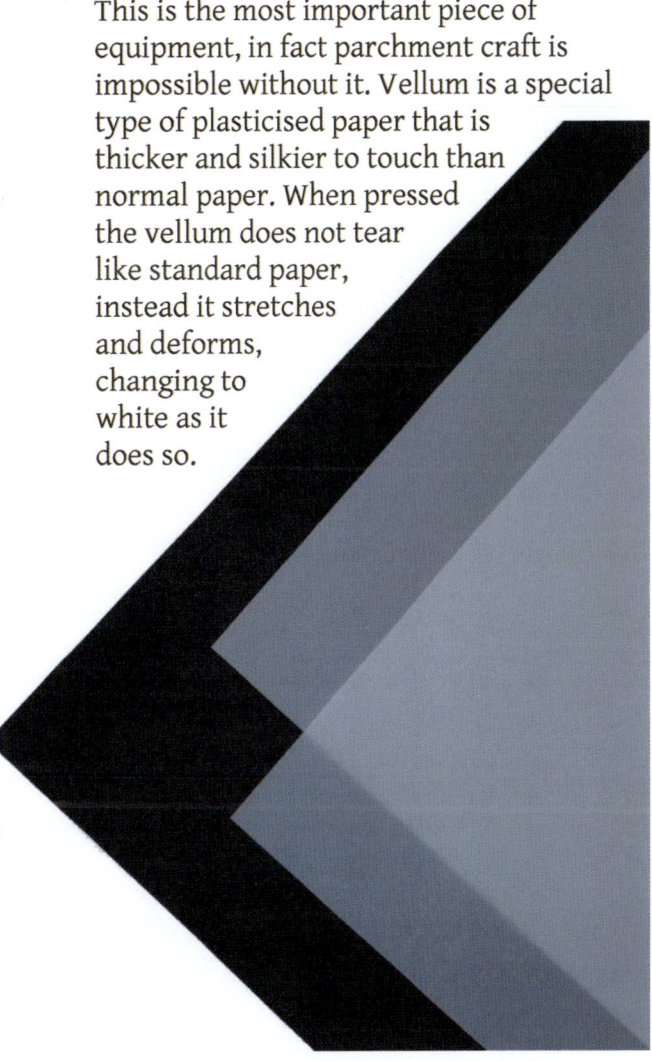

This allows you to create beautiful patterns and effects using the ball tools.

Embossing Mat

The embossing mat is a soft, spongy pad that allows you to emboss the vellum. It should be at least 10mm thick and large enough to use with an A4 pattern. This doesn't necessarily mean you need an A4 mat though, if you purchase a good quality mat you can easily get by with an A5 one. My personal favourite is the Pergamano deluxe embossing/perforating pad. The black colouring makes your embossing much easier to see and the flex in the mat is especially suitable for achieving different shades. Avoid any mat which has a cardboard base as these tend to be too firm for detailed embossing.

White Pencil

Any good quality white pencil will do, so long as it can be sharpened to a fine point. Try to buy an individual pencil from an artist supply shop, rather than using a pencil from a child's colouring set. Children's pencil crayons are too hard and can be difficult to rub away once your embossing is complete, while a quality pencil is much easier to remove.

Black Fine Liner

You will need a black fine liner with a nib no more than 0.4mm thick.

White Wax

Vellum can have a slightly sticky quality that prevents perfectly smooth embossing. By very carefully rubbing the back of the vellum with white wax - such as a tea light - your ball tools will glide with ease.

Eraser

Necessary for erasing the white pencil marks from the front of the parchment vellum once you have finished all the embossing.

Treat your white pencils with care as they break easily and if you cannot sharpen them finely, then they are as good as useless.

Ball Tools

All the different patterns in this book use just 4 sizes of ball tool. Good quality ball tools are an absolute must, scratchy or uncomfortable tools will either ruin your art or be plain horrible to work with.

Extra-Small
The littlest of the ball tools. Just 1mm in diameter, this tiny tool is used to create sharp claws and smooth outlines. Take care with the extra-small tool as it easily punctures the vellum if used roughly.

Small
The standard ball tool. The 1.5mm ball is perfect for creating detailed or fine fur, and small details such as bird feet.

Large
The large ball tool is the go between. The 3.5mm ball is perfect for shading areas which are too fiddly for the extra-large ball tool. It is also the perfect blending tool, allowing you to merge a fine sharp line into a softly shaded area.

Extra-Large
The largest of the ball tools. The 6mm ball can be trickier to wield than the others as it easily goes over lines. But the large size is perfect for the very gentle shading used on backgrounds and large feathers.

Don't Forget a Ruler Too...
Necessary for the borders.

And that's it. With these very easily acquired tools you can make every single project in this book.

Creating Fur and Feathers

...and the other bits of embossing too...

Learning to Emboss

On the bigger projects like the Macaw below there are lots of different techniques combined. The image uses shading, fur flicks and shadow feathers.

All these different effects are created using the four ball tools listed in the tools and materials chapter.

The different sizes of ball tool have different effects – the smaller the ball the more precise but scratchy the effect, while large tools are more subtle and can be blended smoothly together to create gentle shades.

Fur – Mastering the Flick

The first bit of shading you need to master is the 'flick', as this is how fur is created.

To make a 'flick' – press your ball tool into the parchment to make a strongly white spot, then gently flick to one side.

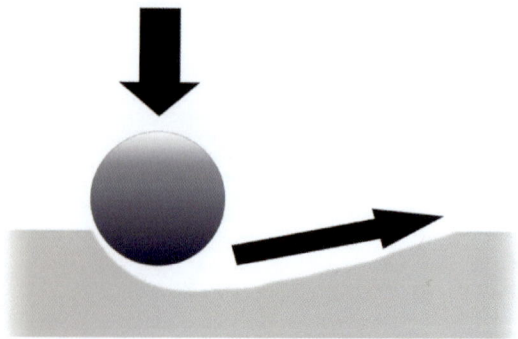

This is a great way to make little flowers, or whiskers on kittens or flashes of light, and can of course just be used as straight forward shading if you line the flicks up so

10

that they make a continuous whole instead of individual marks. If you combine the use of a small ball tool to make the initial flick, then use a larger tool over the top you will end up with a very gently graduating flick with a long soft tail.

Each of the four tools will give you a very different type of flick as can be seen below.

When you are embossing your fur try to keep the flicks in groups or tufts, as this looks much more natural.

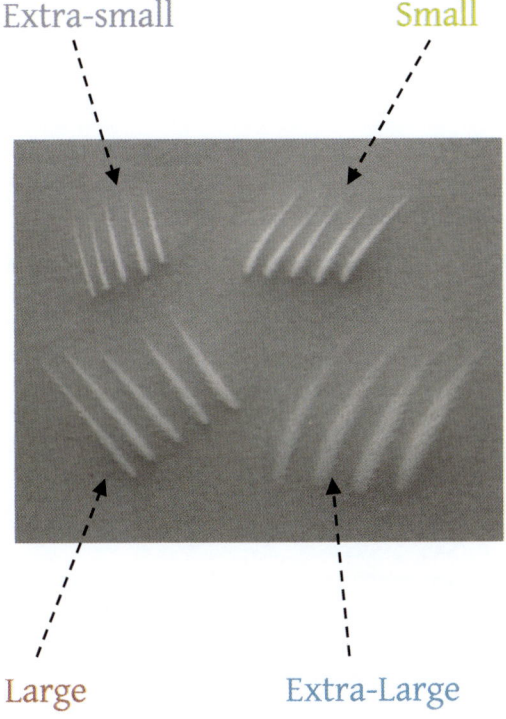

Extra-small   Small

Large   Extra-Large

Generally speaking it's the extra-small and small tools which are used to create fur. The large and extra-large come into their own when you are shading feathers or the very soft fur of cats.

Furry not Regimented

When you are embossing your fur try to keep the flicks in groups or tufts, as this looks much more natural.

Furry Tufts

Soldiers

Feathers – Mastering Smooth

Feathers are more complicated than fur as each feather needs to be treated as an individual.

Unless stated, generally all the feathers are embossed in the same way; using the same tools for the same parts. The aim is to make the feather sharp at the edges but perfectly smooth in the middle.

Which Tools To Use For Which Parts of the Feather

This example uses a close up on some of the feathers from the Macaw.

Extra – Small Ball Tool.

Used to outline the feathers making the edges nice and sharp.

Small Ball Tool.

Used to blend the inside edge of the outline into the body of the feather.

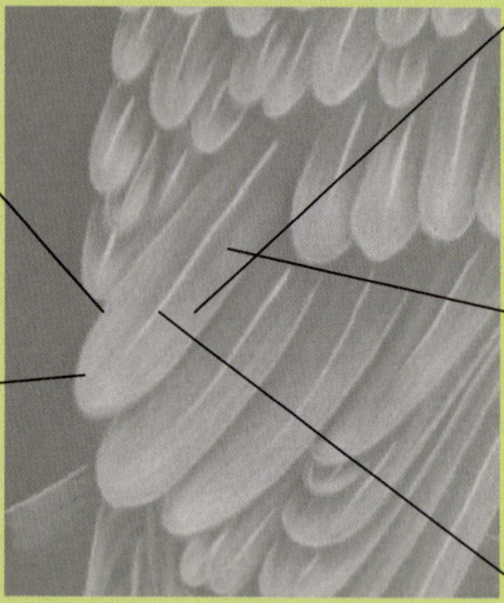

Large Ball Tool.

Blends the middle of the feather.

Extra-Large Ball Tool

Gently shades the embossing up to the next feather.

The Extra-small ball tool is used to make the feather shaft.

How to Create Smooth Embossing

You can create a smoothly shaded effect by very gently pressing the large or extra-large ball tool into the parchment and dragging it across the surface with an even pressure.

By going over the same area repeatedly you will increase the strength of the white. Larger tools will build up slowly and create the very smoothest effect, so always use the largest tool possible for the job. The extra-small and small tools are almost impossible to emboss smoothly with.

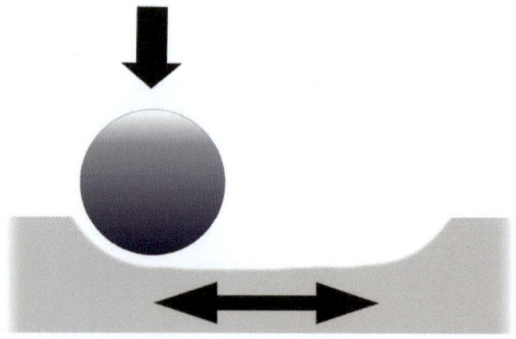

Red Templates Explained

Red templates are used solely to make your life easier. Not everyone has studied how the fur flows over a tiger's nose and these templates mean you don't have to. They show fur length, density and direction.

What Are Red Templates?

On some of the templates in this book you will notice little red lines as well as the black outline; such as those shown on the squirrel below.

Why Use Red in Templates?

The red lines on the templates are there to guide you when embossing fur; helping you to achieve the most realistic image possible. They do this by showing several things such as fur direction, fur density and hair length. All of these characteristics

would be extremely difficult to describe in words - so instead they are put on to the template itself in red.

For example, on the squirrel you can see that the fur on the face and belly is very short, while that on the rest of the body is much longer. This is shown by the length of the little red lines on these parts.

You can also see that the fur is less dense on the belly, compared to the back and that the fur curves along the cheeks.

How to Use Red Templates

The individual project you are working on will have specific instructions on which tool to use for which parts and advice on what effect you are trying to achieve.

Have a go at the example here.

This project is completed using only the small ball tool.

Trace the template using a white pencil.

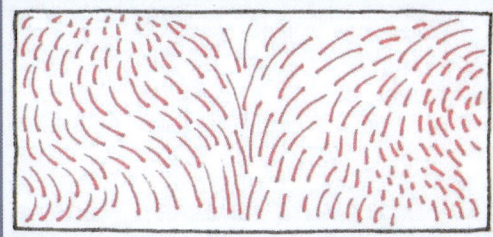

Turn the parchment over and use the small ball tool to emboss the fur, following the lengths and directions shown.

You should have something like this.

Note the finished image is a mirror of the template.

It's All In The Eyes

Mini Project

I cannot stress how important the eyes are. Think of anytime you have been to a zoo. What's the first part of any animal that you look at, what draws your attention. It's almost invariably the eyes, and this is the effect you want your parchment to have.

Cat's Eye Challenge

STEP 1. Trace the black areas of the template using a black fine liner pen on to the parchment vellum.

Fill in the areas so that they are solidly black.

Do not turn the vellum over after tracing. Very lightly go over the traced area with white wax, this will make embossing much easier.

STEP 2. Iris. Use the large ball-tool to emboss the iris so that it is most strongly white just beneath the point of the pupil. Build the embossing up slowly, very gently pressing the ball into the vellum and lightly flicking around the iris.

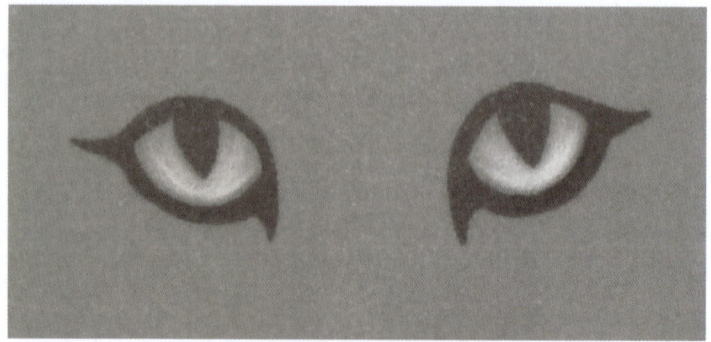

Remember – you can always add more embossing if it needs to be whiter, but you can't take any away once it's there.

STEP 3. Glint. The glint is the scariest part of the whole image because you need to do it in one continuous flick. The glints must ALWAYS be in exactly the same place and be the same shape on both eyes – in this case a curve from left to right along the top edge of the eye.

Use the extra-small ball tool to add the glint to your cat's eyes.

Where possible the glint must also always go over the pupil. You can see clearly the difference the glint makes – it adds life to the otherwise flat eye. The glint is what brings the eye to life, making it look glassy and focussed.

STEP 4. Fur. Only the large ball tool is used to create the fur in this parchment craft image.

Always start with a line of white embossing above the eyes as this will offset the black lines and make the eyes look deeper.

The rest of the fur you can build up slowly around the eyes. Leave gaps in the fur to look like shadows and tufts.

The most important objective with eyes is that the iris is smoothly embossed and the glints are sharp and very white – this is how you get a glassy effect. But eyes are also the most difficult part of creating parchment animals, once you've mastered them, the rest will just fall into place.

CAT'S EYE TEMPLATE

Tips and Tricks

Parchment craft is much the same as any other art form. It takes practice and more than a few mistakes before you get the hang of it. I've made every mistake in the book, so this section is here to help you avoid the usual pitfalls associated with parchment craft.

White Wax

Lightly rub the back of your vellum with white wax – such as a tealight – before you start embossing. This will make the embossing much smoother and easier.

Original Image

Keep referring back to the completed image as you make your parchment craft.

Also keep turning the vellum over to see how the art is coming along.

Water and Heat

Vellum hates both heat and water. If even slightly damp the vellum will distort and bend, while excess heat – such as a heat gun – will blister the vellum. Both rendering it useless.

Smallest Tool First

Always start with the smallest tool and work your way up. This way you reduce the risk of going over the lines, and you keep the edges nice and sharp.

Eyes First

You can make a real mess of an image and get away with it if you get the eyes right. But the opposite is true if you get the eyes wrong. For this reason always start with the eyes.

Read the Instructions

It may seem basic – but make sure you read the instructions *thoroughly* before you begin.

This way you won't get any nasty surprises.

These are just a few thoughts to help you with your parchment crafting. By far the most important thing for you to do now is practice, experiment and above all have fun creating your masterpieces.

Parchment Craft – Embossing Art Volume 1.

Tiger Cub Pattern

Pattern 1. Eagles

Eagles Template

Eagles

You will need:

- Vellum and embossing mat
- White pencil
- Extra-small ball tool
- Small ball tool
- Large ball tool
- Extra-large ball tool
- Ruler

Trace
Trace the entire image using a sharp white pencil. Do not trace the red lines on the perching eagle's head as these lines are only there to indicate feather length and direction.

Embossing
All embossing is completed on the SAME SIDE as the tracing. When you are ready to begin embossing place your vellum onto the embossing mat.

Use the extra-small ball tool and a ruler to emboss the outer border. Try to do this in one single line so that the border is smooth without any jerks or wiggles in it.

> **PERCHING EAGLE**
>
> This eagle is the main focus of the image and so needs to be completed in the most detail.
>
> Make sure the edges of all the feathers are nice and sharp, and try not to go over the lines when embossing the beak.

Face
All the feathers on the face start at the beak and then flow smoothly back over the bird's head and neck.

Use the extra-small ball tool to emboss the tiny feathers on the eagle's face. Start just behind the beak and press the tool lightly into the vellum then flick in the desired direction to create a short line. These feathers are represented by the red lines on the template. The length and direction of the red lines indicate how long your flicks should be and in which direction they should go. Please note you will need to complete more flicks than are shown on the template otherwise your eagle will look bald.

Use the large ball tool to add a pale line above the eagle's eye; where the brow is. This will make the eagle's eyes look more deeply set.

Use the extra-small ball tool to add the tiny dots in front of and behind the eagle's eye.

Eye
As with all animals the eagle's eye is the most important part of the design. It is the first area of focus for the viewer, and the most interesting. Take your time completing the eye, practicing before hand

on a separate piece of vellum if you feel you need to.

Use the extra-small ball tool to gently go over the outline of both the iris and the pupil.

Use the small ball tool to very carefully shade the inside of the iris so that it is strongly white at the base and fades as it gets closer to the pupil.

Keep looking at the completed image to help you.

The embossing on the iris needs to be as smooth as possible so work slowly, gradually building up the white of the eye.

Use the extra-small ball tool to add the glint in the eagle's eye - note this is not shown on the template. The glint is to the left of the pupil, about halfway to the edge of the iris. The glint is a single white line that follows the curve of the eye for about 3mm.

Beak

Use the small ball tool to emboss the lower edge of the upper half of the beak, this needs to be the whitest part of the beak. Use the extra-small ball tool to emboss the tip of the beak so it is nice and sharp.

Use the large ball tool to emboss the rest of the beak so the top is pale white and the lower edge is more strongly white. Shade the two edges together, but leave a gap in the embossing along the lower part of the beak so that the two stand out from each other.

Use the large ball tool to add a line running along the beak towards the tip, starting from just below the nostril - this is a highlight being created by the sun above.

Neck and chest

> The feathers on the neck, shoulders and back are sharp and jagged with no shaft running down the centre.

Use the extra-small ball tool to go over the lines of the feathers on the eagle's neck and chest. Use the small ball tool, then the large ball tool to shade the feathers so that they are very strongly white at the tip and this fades up to the next feather. Leave a gap in the embossing before you reach the next set of feathers. This gap will help the bird to look a bit rougher and more 3D.

Wings and tail

These feathers are completed the same way as the neck; using the extra-small ball tool to make the edges sharp and the small, then large, ball tool to fade this white edge back up to the next feather. These feathers differ in that they are individual, whereas the neck and back feathers were grouped together. To show the individuality of the wing feathers you must leave a tiny gap between them, not allowing any feather to touch another.

The longest wing feathers are completed using the large ball tool by embossing along the lines on the template. Try not to go over the lines so that the end of the wing is sharp. If you find this difficult you may wish to use the small ball tool – but do so gently as you don't want the tip of the wing to be too white. Once you have embossed the lines, use the large ball tool to very lightly shade between the gaps in the lines.

The wing and tail feathers also have a shaft running down the center. This is embossed using the extra-small ball tool in one long continuous flick down the middle of the feather. Press the tool into the vellum and flick in the desired direction. Be aware that the faster you do this the smoother the flick will be, but you will have less control over the length and direction.

Legs and feet

The back of the legs is completed in exactly the same way as the feathers on the neck.

The rest of the legs are completed using only the large ball tool.; just the same as with the face, the legs are comprised of long fur-style flicks. The upper edge of the leg is almost white, but the rest of the leg is much more muted. Leave a large gap of roughly 3mm between the leg fur flicks and the wing feathers so that they stand out from each other.

Use the extra-small ball tool to go over the lines of the feet and talons. Use the large ball tool to shade just the top of the feet and use the extra-small ball tool to add a cluster of very light dots to the pads on the base of each of the toes.

> ## FLYING EAGLE
> The flying eagle is much further away than the perching one, and so doesn't need to be as detailed. It is more like a representation of a flying eagle, rather than a detailed example of one.

Body

The body is completed using the extra-small ball tool to create the same fur flicks as used on the perching eagle's head. The jagged lines on the template represent where the fur flicks need to be the strongest and whitest.

Use the extra-small ball tool to go around the eagle's eye.

Use the small ball tool to emboss the beak so that it is white at the end and fades towards the face.

Emboss the feet with the small ball tool so that they are strongly and evenly white.

Wings and tail

The wings and tail feathers are completed the same way as the wings of the perching eagle, only smaller. Take care using the large ball tool on the smaller feathers as it is very easy to go over the lines and this would blur your eagle.

Rocks

Use the extra-small ball tool to go over the outlines of the rocks and grass so that they are strongly white.

Use the large ball tool to emboss the rocks themselves. Place the tool on the edge of a rock and flick towards the centre. Try to keep all the rock flicks perfectly straight and parallel to the horizontal border at the bottom of the picture. Use this to fill all the edges of the rocks, but leave some gaps in the embossing to look like shadow. Then use the tool in a gentle side-to-side motion to fill in any large gaps. On the furthest rock emboss only the outside edge. Use the small ball tool to emboss the grass at the bottom of the picture strongly white.

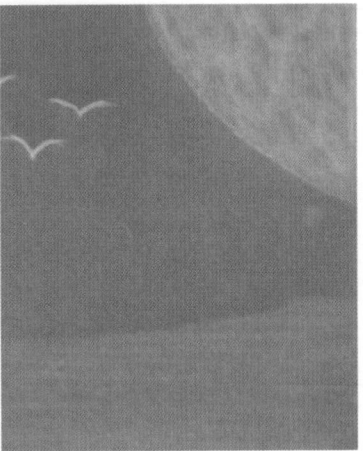

Background

Use the extra-small ball tool to emboss the distant birds.

Use the extra-large ball tool to emboss the clouds and sun. The clouds are completed using a side-to-side motion to very lightly fill the entire area. Try to keep the clouds as smooth as possible. The sun is completed by using the extra-large ball tool in a circular motion to fill in the area. The sun is more strongly white than the clouds but still faint in comparison to the eagles.

To create the hills follow the same direction as for the clouds, but this time also use the large ball tool to add a very faint line at the top of each hill so that it looks like the sun is shining on them. Be sure to fade this line back into the rest of the hill embossing.

Pattern 2. Harvest Mice

Harvest Mice Template.

Harvest Mice

> To complete this project you will need:
> - Vellum and embossing mat
> - Sharp white pencil
> - Black fine liner
> - Extra-small ball tool
> - Small ball tool
> - Large ball tool

Tracing

Trace the black lines of the template with the white pencil, but don't trace the red lines, these are there to guide you when you are embossing the fur. Use the black fine liner to fill in the eyes but make sure you leave the little glint in each eye – these can be seen on the template.

Do not turn the parchment over, all embossing is completed on the same side as the black eyes.

> **DON'T FORGET**
>
> Rub the back of the parchment vellum very gently with white wax before you begin embossing – this will make shading much easier.

Embossing

Place the vellum on to the embossing mat.

Use the small ball tool to emboss all the mice fingers and toes so that they are strongly white. You want these to stand out just as much as the eyes on the completed image, to do this the fingers will need to be as white as possible without damaging the vellum.

The Mice

All the mice are completed in exactly the same way – using the same tools for the same body parts.

Ears

Use the large ball tool to go over the lines of the ears to create a C shape.

Fur

All the fur, on all the mice, is completed using the extra-small ball tool.

Follow the red template. The red lines on the template are showing you fur length and direction. Where the lines are short; so must yours be, and where they are longer; so must yours be. For example, the fur on the top of the head is short while that on the belly is longer.

Pay particular attention to shadowy areas on the mice; such as under the arms and the belly.

To create the shadow, these areas need less embossing; that is fewer fur flicks with a slightly greater distance between each individual flick. These shadow flicks also need to be fainter than the rest of the body embossing.

Again, don't forget to keep referring back to your completed image.

Complete the whiskers in one confident flick with the extra-small ball tool.

Using the large ball tool shade the tails of the mice so that the **right hand side is more strongly white than the left.** Use the small ball tool to make sure the end of the tail is nice and sharp.

Use the large ball tool to emboss the two lower mice's noses solidly white.

Wheat

Use the extra-small ball tool to go over the outline on each bud of wheat. But ONLY on the right hand side. Use the large ball tool to shade the rest of each individual bud by placing the tool on the line you just embossed, and gently flicking into the bud. Repeat this until you have filled each individual bud before moving on to the next one. Keep this embossing rough so that you can see lines, this will create a different texture. Leave a very slight gap between each bud to separate it from its neighbours.

Use the large ball tool to gently shade the stalks of wheat. These are very pale compared to the rest of the picture.

Use the large ball tool to emboss the blades of grass. Use the tool to create long lines of embossing that run the entire length of the grass and slowly build up the lines until most of the leaf is covered. Leave a few gaps between the lines; these will act as shadow. Also, leave a gap in the leaf embossing under each of the mice to create their shadows.

Pattern 3. Howling Wolf

Howling Wolf
Template

Howling Wolf

Unlike many of the other patterns, the Howling Wolf is ideal if you don't have a lot of time. You can create an effective and atmospheric pattern - that looks like it took a lot longer than it did - in about an hour.

Tracing
Trace and colour the black part of the template with a black fine liner. If you have a black felt tip handy you can use this instead to save time.

Trace the moon with the white pencil.

Remember – Always trace on a solid surface, such as a table, then place the vellum on the embossing mat when you are ready to emboss.

Embossing
Do not turn the vellum over – all embossing is completed on the same side as the black coloring.

BE VERY CAREFULL – any embossing will show through the black on the front of the vellum.

> To create this project you will need:
> - Vellum and embossing mat
> - Black fine liner
> - Black felt tip (optional)
> - White pencil
> - Extra-large ball tool
> - Large ball tool
> - Small ball tool
> - Extra-small ball tool

So be careful not to go into the black areas of the template when you are embossing.

Moon
Use the extra-large ball tool to emboss the moon. Use the tool in tiny circles to slowly fill in the whole area of the moon. Be careful not to go over any of the black.

If you find the extra-large too cumbersome, you may wish to use the large ball tool to emboss the small gaps between the branches and to go around the wolf.

Try to make the whole moon evenly white.

DO NOT be tempted to go over any of the outlines before you emboss the moon. If you do you will never get rid of these lines and that will ruin the effect. Keep turning your vellum over to see how your embossing is progressing, if any one area is too pale, work on that until it matches the rest of the moon.

Stars

Use the extra-small ball tool to cover the whole sky in a random arrangement of little tiny dots. Vary the size of these dots so that a few a slightly larger, these will look like brighter or closer stars.

Use the small ball tool to add the little beams coming from a few of the stars. Gently press the tool in to the centre of the star then flick outwards . Complete four flicks for each of the stars.

Border
This is the only part of the pattern which is surprisingly tricky. Take your time placing the ruler before you start to emboss and don't forget you can not rub out embossing – once it's there, it's there for good!

Place the ruler on the black outline.
Draw one line with the extra-small ball tool and then immediately follow with the large ball tool. You will find this creates a double border.

Pattern 4. Macaw

Macaw Template

The Macaw

To complete this project you will need:

- Vellum and embossing mat
- White pencil
- Black fine liner
- Extra-small ball tool
- Small ball tool
- Large ball tool
- Extra-large ball tool

It's pretty, but...

DO NOT START WITH THIS PATTERN

The macaw is just about the most complicated pattern in this book, and if you start here, you are asking for frustration.

If you are looking for your first pattern go for the humming bird instead, he's just as good looking and will give you plenty of practice before you take on the biggy...

Tracing
Trace the entire template with a white pencil

Turn the vellum over, then colour the eye and beak parts in black with the black fine liner.

Once you are ready to emboss, place the vellum on to the embossing mat.

Embossing
All the embossing is completed on the **same side** as the black fine liner.

Beak
Use the extra-small ball tool to outline the beak, being very careful to not go into the black area as this will show on the front of the vellum.

Use the small ball tool to emboss the tip of the beak, then use the large ball tool to emboss the rest of the beak using the tool in long lines to create a smooth effect. The beak needs to be whitest next to the black area as can be seen in the image right.

Use the large ball tool to emboss the lower half of the beak so that it is smooth and very pale white. Remember, you won't be able to see your embossing as you are working on black, so work slowly, and keep turning the vellum over to check your progress.

Remember - it's okay to leave areas with no embossing at all.

Head
Use the extra-small ball tool to emboss the feathers on the top of the head. The feathers right next to the beak are strongly white; this embeds the beak in the bird's head – otherwise it will look like it's

floating!

Just like fur, these feathers are completed using the tool to create a tiny flick. Where there are jagged lines on the template around the back of the parrot's head is where the fur flicks need to be the whitest.

By graduating how strongly white the feathers are, you will create shadows which in turn make the bird look more 3D and realistic.

Complete these feather flicks on top of the bird's head and down the back of its neck.

Eye
Use the extra-small ball tool to very lightly go around the eye, and to add the tiny glint as well. Use the small ball tool to VERY gently add the tiny pale reflection line running at the base of the eye. Be really careful here, as you can not see what you are doing in the black, but your embossing will show on the front of the parchment.

Face
Use the extra-large ball tool to emboss the face. Use the tool in tiny circles and very slowly fill in the area of the face. Don't go into the eye, feathers or beak. Leave the face embossing slightly patchy.

Within this area of patchy white use the extra-small ball tool to add dots - just where the skin of the face is showing.

Feathers
All the feathers on the macaw's back and wings are completed in the same way – all you are varying is the size.

Use the extra-small ball tool to emboss over the line so that each feather has a distinctive edge.

Use the small ball tool to emboss the tip of each feather strongly white, then use the large tool to fade this embossing up the length of the feather.

Look at the completed image; all feathers have a shadow in the embossing before the start of the next feather. By leaving a shadow each feather stands out from the next, making it look like they are all equally important.

This attention to detail will improve the overall effect of your bird.

35

Once the body of the feathers is completed you need to add the central shaft to each individual feather. Use the extra-small ball tool to add a single strong white line running down the center of each feather- this needs to be straight and smooth to be effective.

The shafts on the wings are tricky as they are much longer than those on the body, take your time and practice on a scrap piece of vellum before you start on the bird itself.

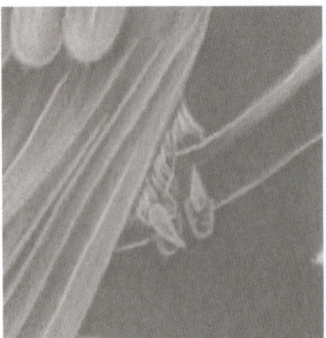

Foot
Use the small ball tool to emboss the claws solidly white.

Use the small ball tool to add the little tufts of feather flicks along the bird's ankle.

KEY POINTS ON THE MACAW

Smooth
The feathers are the main show for this pattern and to be effective they must be as smooth as possible.

Shadow
The shadows on the bird create the 3D effect, if you forget to put the shadows in your macaw will look flat and cartoon-like.

Straight
If the shafts of your feathers curve or look a bit wobbly it will ruin the effect. Practice creating straight shafts with the extra-small ball tool before you work on the actual bird.

Tail

The tail is completed in a slightly different way compared to the wing and body feathers.

Complete the outline and tail tip the same as the body feathers, but then use the large ball tool to create a more striated effect running up the length of the tail feathers. Place the ball on the edge of the feather and flick gently UP + TOWARDS the centre of the feather. See the image left. Leave gaps in your embossing so that on the completed feather you can see the shadows. Once you have completed the edges, add the shaft exactly the same as you did on the wings – using the extra-small ball tool in one long continuous flick down the center.

The comparison between the stylized nature of the leaves compared with the rest of the image works well as it draws the viewers eye to different parts of the image. So don't be tempted to add veins to the leaves – leave them pure.

Once you have completed the branch give your macaw one last check over – particularly making sure all the feathers have shafts as these are easily neglected.

Leaves
Use the extra-small ball tool to very gently go over all the outlines of the background leaves.

Use the small ball tool to make the tip of each of the leaves strongly white, then use the large and extra-large ball tools to shade the leaf back towards the branch.

Take your time and try to make both sides of each leaf evenly white.

Branch
Use the small ball tool to emboss the tip of the branch strongly white. Then use the large ball tool to emboss only the TOP surface of the branch a muted white.

In this pattern, the macaw is very much the star of the show –the last thing you want is for the background to standout more than the bird does. Keep the branch embossing muted and only the very tips of the leaves can be bright white.

37

Pattern 5. Tiger Cub

Tiger cub template

Tiger cub

Tracing

Trace the whole tiger using a white pencil. Then use the black fine liner to colour all the black parts of the template, including the stripes, eyes, and ears.

Embossing

Once you have traced your tiger, place the vellum onto the embossing mat.

All the embossing is completed on the **same side as the black stripes** – this is so when viewed from the front the fur will appear to be over the black stripes.

To complete this project you will need:

- Vellum
- Embossing mat
- White pencil
- Black fine liner
- Extra-small ball tool
- Small ball tool
- Large ball tool
- Extra-large ball tool

Eyes

The tiger's eyes are embossed in exactly the same way as those on the cat's eye challenge.

Use the large ball tool to emboss the iris so that it is whitest just below the pupil and fades towards the top of the eye.

Use the extra-small ball tool to add the tiny glint in the top of the pupil and to add a line of white that curves along the top of the iris – starting in the pupil and running towards the back of the eye.

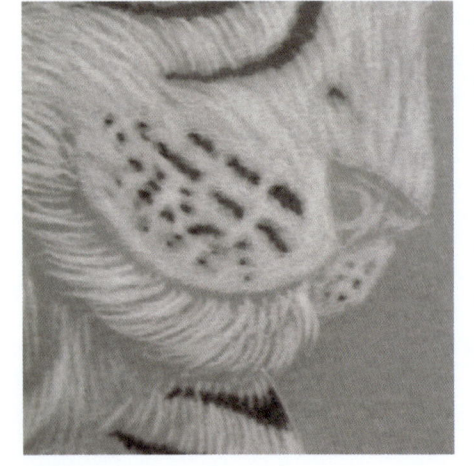

Muzzle

Use the large ball tool to emboss the cub's muzzle.

Use the tool in tiny circles and fill in the area around the whisker spots. Try to keep this embossing as smooth as possible. Make sure your embossing does not go over

40

the black spots - otherwise it will cover the black on the front of the image and the cub will look like he has no whiskers.

Fur

Once you have traced the template this pattern is all about fur.

The red lines on the template represent the fur on the tiger and will guide you in both fur length and direction. For example the fur on the tiger's head is very short while that on the cheeks is much longer. Try not to emboss the tiger's fur in neat lines, instead group the hair into tufts. This will look much more natural.

Use the small ball tool to emboss the fur on the tiger's face and chin. Complete each individual hair by pressing the ball into the vellum and flicking in the desired direction.

When completing the fur, follow the template closely and keep turning the vellum over to see how you are progressing.

Creating Perfect Stripes

Allow your fur embossing to go over the black stripes of the tiger (but NOT the eye area). This will help the stripes to look like coloured fur, and naturally part of the cat rather than just painted on.

Use the large ball tool to go over the fur on the top of the tiger's head, and over the back of the tiger's neck. By using the larger tool you will make this fur look smoother and silkier than the rest. Of course, if you want an ultra-smooth tiger you can emboss all the fur with the large ball tool - but I prefer tiger cubs to look a little scruffy.

Leave a gap around the tiger's cheeks and chin when you are embossing the body fur, as you want these parts to stand out.

Note how the fur changes direction as it comes down from the tiger's shoulders and sweeps around to the chest. When completing this fur, remember to keep moving the vellum so that you are always comfortable.

The fur also changes texture on the chest. Leave larger gaps between the tufts and allow some of the hairs to stick out in random directions.

When you reach the last black stripe on the cub's back, make sure you continue to emboss fur for another couple of centimetres –at the same time allowing the fur embossing to get fainter and fainter as you do so. This way, it will look like there is more tiger in the distance and the cub doesn't just abruptly stop.

Use the small ball tool to add a few tiny flicks coming out from the back of the tiger's neck to make the cub look a bit scruffier.

Nose

Use the large ball tool to very lightly go over just the lines on the cub's nose. Leave the rest of the nose free of embossing.

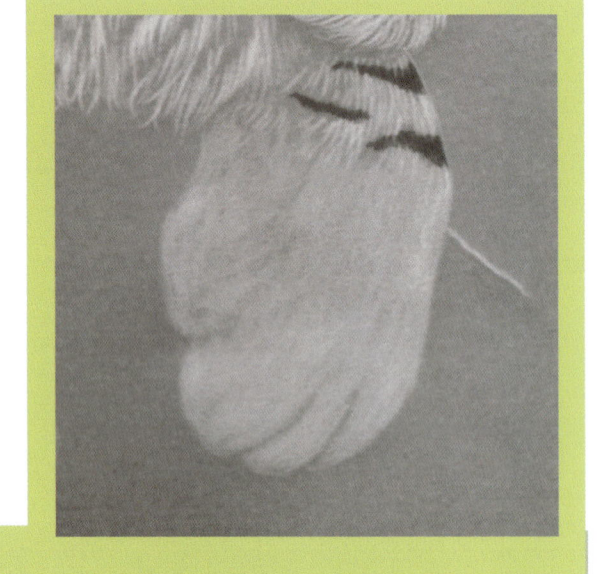

Paws

Use the extra-large ball tool to emboss the cub's feet. Use the tool in a very small circular motion and gradually add layers of embossing, very slowly building up the white as smoothly as possible. You want the paws to look velvety soft.

Leave a tiny gap in the embossing between the toes so they are separated from each other.

Blend this smooth embossing up the leg to just behind the rest of the body fur. You want this smooth embossing and the rougher fur to merge together without a noticeable join.

Background

Use the extra-small ball tool to emboss over the outline of the rock the cub is lying on. Leave the rest of the rock free of embossing so that the cub is the only subject the viewer focuses on.

Practice, Practice, Practice

So, now you've had a taste of what parchment craft has to offer. Just remember, parchment craft is an ART. It takes dedication and practice to get things right.

Remember these tips from before...

White Wax

Lightly rub the back of your vellum with white wax – such as a tealight – before you start embossing. This will make the embossing much smoother and easier.

Original Image

Keep referring back to the completed image as you make your parchment craft.

Also keep turning the vellum over to see how the art is coming along.

Water and Heat

Vellum hates both heat and water. If even slightly damp the vellum will distort and bend, while excess heat – such as a heat gun – will blister the vellum. Both rendering it useless.

Smallest Tool First

Always start with the smallest tool and work your way up. This way you reduce the risk of going over the lines and you keep the edges nice and sharp.

Eyes First

You can make a real mess of an image and get away with it if you get the eyes right. But the opposite is true if you get the eyes wrong. For this reason always start with the eyes.

Read the Instructions

It may seem basic – but make sure you read the instructions *thoroughly* before you begin.

This way you won't get any nasty surprises.

...They really will help you with your parchment crafting. By far the most important thing for you to do now is practice, experiment and above all have fun creating your masterpieces.

Pattern 6. Rock Dragon

Rock Dragon Template

Rock Dragon

I like my little rock dragon to have a slightly rough appearance; the lines are a bit scruffy and the embossing is not too smooth. I imagine he's a bit of a cheeky dragon.

Trace
Trace the entire image using a sharp white pencil.
Turn the vellum over and using the black fine liner fill in the dragon's eye.

Once you are ready to emboss, place the vellum on to the embossing mat.

Embossing
All the embossing is completed on the SAME side as the black fine liner.

Use the extra-small ball tool to go over all the lines of the image so that they are strongly white.

Head
Using the extra-small ball tool very carefully add the tiny glint to the dragon's eye - including the gently circular sweep that curves around the lower edge of the eye. This will give the eye a nice round shape.

Remember to turn the parchment vellum over frequently to see how your image is coming along, and to make any changes that might be necessary.

To create this project you will need:
- Vellum and embossing mat
- White pencil and black fine liner
- Extra-small ball tool
- Small ball tool
- Large ball tool
- Extra-large ball tool

This is one for you to play with;

If you want to add spots - then do so, if you think the dragon should have fur, then go ahead, what's stopping you? Dragons are a great subject to practise new techniques on, and at the same time just have a bit of fun with your crafting.

Use the small ball tool to emboss around the eye so that the embossing next to the black is very white, and this fades rapidly into the rest of the head. All the flanges and points on the head, around the jaws and eyes are embossed with the small ball tool; making the tips very strongly white and then fading this in to the rest of the head with the large ball tool.

Use the large ball tool to emboss along the lower edge of the jaw and to make the dragon's muzzle white. Leave a gap in the embossing around the muzzle. Use the extra-small ball tool to emboss the teeth strongly white.

Use the extra-small ball tool to emboss the tips of the crest on the dragon's head strongly white and sharp. Using first the small, then the large ball tool, gradually fade this down towards the dragon's head. Use the large ball tool to add the curved bulge at the base of each of the larger crest spines.

There is a very fine membrane between the crests. Use the large ball tool to very lightly fill this with smooth embossing, leaving just a narrow gap along the edge of the spines.

Don't emboss any of the little scales on the dragon's face; instead use the extra-small ball tool to add a line along the center of each scale.

Wings

Use the small ball tool to emboss the four fingers of the wing as strongly white as you can, without piercing the vellum. Take care here as this is the part where you are most likely to accidentally puncture the vellum.

The membrane of the wing needs to look like it's slightly see-through and fragile.

Use the small ball tool and press it lightly into the edge of one of the membranes - right next to one of the wing fingers. Flick the tool towards the centre of the wing following the curve of the outer edge. Repeat this up and down the edge of the membrane. Leave gaps in the embossing so that the membrane is not solid, and has the appearance of shadows.

Use the large ball tool to add a slightly stronger line to the very edge of the wing membrane.

The wing arm is embossed using the large ball tool so that the outside edge is strongly white, while the inside edge is pale.

Use the extra-small ball tool to emboss the tip of the wing claw very strongly white. Try to keep this as sharp as possible. Use the small ball tool to shade the inner edge of the claw white and leave a shadow on the upper edge, as can be seen on the left.

Body

The same with on the face, don't emboss any of the tiny scales on the dragon's body, instead just use the extra-small ball tool to add a single line that runs along the centre of each scale.

Use the large ball tool to fill in the gaps between the scales. Use the tool in a simple zigzag motion – like you would with a colouring pencil – to lightly shade the area between the scales - just to make the dragon look solid.

Use this exact same technique on the dragon's back leg, which you can just see poking out above the rock. The leg should be very slightly stronger white than the rest of the body as it is closer to the viewer.

The ridge running along the dragon's back stands out much more than the rest of the body. Use the small ball tool to emboss the point of each ridge scale so that it is white and then use the small and large ball tools to bring this embossing down along the edge of the ridge scale.
You want the edge of each scale to be strongly white so that the embossing blends with the tracing line you made earlier. Fade this embossing back towards the next scale, but leave a gap in the embossing before you get to this next scale.

Keep referring to the completed image as a guide, and repeat this on all the ridge scales along the dragon's back.

Feet

Leave the claws completely free of embossing.

Use the small ball tool to emboss the top and bottom of each toe, gently fading this back towards the centre of the toe.

Tail

Use the small, then large ball tool, to emboss the tail fluke so that the outer edge is very strongly white and this fades towards the central part. Use the small ball tool to shade the inner part of the tail fluke, this part is very close to the viewer and so needs to be the strongest white of the whole image.

Use the large ball tool to shade the rest of the tail. The upper most edge of the tail is the strongest white and there is a shadow that runs along the bottom. Don't forget that where the tail curves over the rocks the position of the shadow will change. Use the completed image as a guide.

Use the large ball tool to make the outermost edge of the tail's curve softly white, this part of the tail would be in shadow but if you leave it clear of embossing then it makes the tail look a strange shape.

Leave the grass completely clear of embossing.

Rocks

Use the large ball tool to complete the rocks. If you look at the image above you will notice that all the rocks are embossed using nothing more than straight lines. To work, these lines need to run parallel to the bottom of your image and all be perfectly in line with each other. Use the large ball tool in soft straight strokes, gradually building up the whiteness. The right hand side of each rock is more strongly white than the left. Leave a gap in the rock embossing around any grass, dragon or other rocks that you get close to. The lines on the left side of the rocks, and those under the dragon's tail are very light as they are only there to show that the ground is solid.

DON'T FORGET

White Wax

Lightly rub the back of your vellum with white wax – such as a tealight – before you start embossing. This will make the embossing much smoother and easier.

Smallest Tool First

Always start with the smallest tool and work your way up. This way you reduce the risk of going over the lines and you keep the edges nice and sharp.

Pattern 7. Pegasus

Pegasus Template

Pegasus

To complete this project you will need:

- Vellum and mat
- White pencil
- Extra-small ball tool
- Small ball tool
- Extra-large ball tool
- Large ball tool
- White wax (optional)

Tracing:
Trace the entire template using the sharp white pencil.

Embossing:
Depending on which way you wish Pegasus to be facing you can emboss on either side of the vellum.

Before embossing gently rub the vellum with the white wax - this will help to keep the embossing smooth and easy.

Face and Body.
Pegasus's body and face are embossed using only the extra-large and large ball tools. The shadows in the embossing are just as important as the white areas. Note where the body has shadows in the embossing, such as the long lines where the ribs would be, and try to imitate this in your image. This embossing can be tricky, but if you get it right your Pegasus will look much more realistic. Leave a gap in the embossing around the mane and tail and under the wings. This will allow the whiteness of these parts to really stand out.

Use the extra-large ball tool to complete all the embossing on the body and face then use the large ball tool to increase the whiteness along the top of the chest and neck, along the bottom of the jaw and cheek, along the tops of the front legs, and the front of both back legs.

Pegasus can either be left with a dark eye or it can be lightly embossed with a small ball tool. Do not attempt to emboss the entire eye, as this will leave Pegasus looking blind.

Use the large ball tool to add the white lines running down the center of Pegasus's lower front and back legs.

Mane and Tail:
The mane, tail and wings are the most important part of Pegasus as these parts stand out the most. Take your time and practice on a separate sheet of vellum if necessary.

Use the small ball tool to emboss the tips of each hair segment strongly white and use the extra-small ball tool to make sure the tips themselves are nice and sharp.

Use the large ball tool to fade this embossing back into the body of the tail. Use long gentle strokes with the ball tool to get a really smooth effect. Use the small ball tool to add a few stronger lines flowing in the mane and tail to show these parts are hair.

Use the small ball tool to emboss the tips of the fur on the hooves, ankles and elbows and to emboss the base of each of the hooves. Use the extra-small ball tool to sharpen the edges.

Wings:

Use the small ball tool to emboss around the outside edge of each of the flight feathers on the wing (flight feathers are the big ones). Leaving a slight gap between feathers.

Use the large ball tool, then the extra-large ball tool, to gradually draw this embossing towards the main body of the wing. The embossing of the wings needs to be as smooth as possible with a very gradual reduction in intensity.

Leave a shadow of at least 2mm before the smaller feathers on the body of the wing.
Use the extra-small ball tool to very carefully add the shaft to each of the flight feathers. This should be done in a single flick that runs around three-quarters of the length, down the centre of the feather.

Repeat this process for the little feathers on the body of the wing. Use the small ball tool to emboss along the top edge of the wing so that it is strongly white, as shown right.

Use only the large ball tool to very lightly emboss just the lines of the wing in the background – you don't want this to be anywhere nearly as white as the wing in the foreground.

Pattern 8. Hummingbird

Hummingbird Template

Hummingbird

This is a great pattern to start with if you are new to parchment craft as it uses all the different techniques without being overly complicated.

Tracing

Trace the whole template in the centre of a piece of vellum with the white pencil. Turn the vellum over and use the black fine liner to fill in the black areas you can see on the template – namely the tail, wings and eye. Take your time here and pay close attention to where there are white lines within the black areas of the template.

Wait for the black ink to dry then gently rub over the entire pattern with a piece of white wax, this will make embossing much easier .

To create this project you will need:

- Parchment craft vellum
- Embossing mat
- White pencil
- Black fine liner
- Extra-small ball tool
- Small ball tool
- Large ball tool
- White wax - optional

Once you are ready to emboss, place the vellum onto the embossing mat.

Do NOT turn your parchment over – emboss on the SAME side as the black ink.

Embossing

Use the extra-small ball tool to go over the white lines on the edges of the wings so that they are strongly white. Use the small ball tool to add very faint lines in the black areas of the wings to represent feathers.

Beak

Use the extra-small ball tool to emboss the line that runs along the centre of the beak.

Use the small ball tool to emboss the upper half of the beak so that the tip is strongly white but the rest is a more muted grey. Leave a gap in the embossing in the centre of the upper part of the beak.

Remember to keep referring to the images to help you.

Use the large ball tool to emboss the lower half of the beak, leaving a very slight gap underneath the white line.

Head

Use the small ball tool to create tiny rectangular patches of feathers by joining a series of very short flicks together – the same type of flicks that you use to create fur. Start from the base of the beak and work your way back over the head. Do not emboss in the black area of the eye as this will show on the front and you want the eye to be clear.

You can also use this technique to fill in any gaps between the feathers when you emboss the body.

Use the extra-small ball tool to emboss the tiny glint in the hummingbird's eye.

Body feathers

Go over all the outlines of the body feathers with the extra-small ball tool.

Use the small, then large, ball tools to extend this embossing smoothly back. Leave a paler gap in the centre of each feather so that when you emboss the shaft it really stands out.

You want to create the look of lots of individual feathers. Don't forget the feathers on the hummingbird's face and the tiny ones beneath its chin.

Use the extra-small ball tool to add the shaft down the centre of each of the larger feathers. This needs to be a single flick done with precision and confidence so you may wish to practise on a separate sheet of vellum before you start on the actual bird. Make sure the shaft runs down the centre of the feather, leaving a gap of about 1mm at the top and bottom.

Use the extra-small ball tool to go over the outline of the toes, but don't emboss them.

Use the small ball tool to emboss the underbelly feathers poking down from behind the twig. Create these using the same flick action as you used between the feathers, only this time the feathers are much longer and thicker and so must your flicks be. Make sure you emboss between all of the toes so that these stand out.

Tail

Use the extra-small ball tool to emboss the long thin lines of the tail streamers. To create the hearts, place the tip of the small ball tool on the outside edge of one of the tail hearts and flick in towards the centre of the heart. Repeat this all around the edge, leaving tiny gaps to act as shadows.

Leaves

All the leaves are completed in exactly the same way.

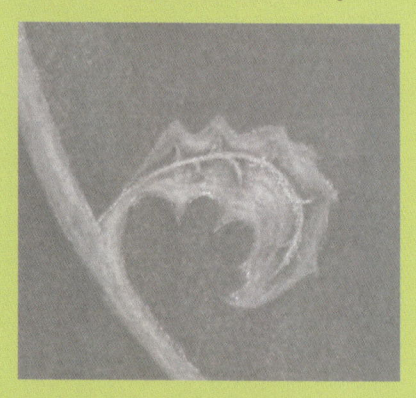

Use the extra-small ball tool to emboss the central lines on each leaf. Then use the large tool to fill in the rest of the leaf so that it is an even muted white. The last thing you want is for the leaves to stand out more than the bird does, so keep them quite a gentle white.

Don't worry if your leaves look a bit scratchy, personally I like to see them a bit rough as they compliment the precision you used in the humming bird.

Twig

Use the large ball tool to very slowly build up the white of the twig. Emboss in long lines and increase the strength of the white slowly, if you rush, the twig will be very patchy or you may even rip the vellum. You want the twig to be evenly white with a slight gap in the embossing beneath the hummingbird.

Flowers

Use the small ball tool to make the tips of each of the petals sharp and strongly white. Use the large ball tool to shade this into the body of the petal.

Less is more with the flowers as you want them to be soft and delicate. Leave a gap between each petal so that they stand out from each other.

Do not be tempted to emboss the outline of the flowers as this will make them appear very cartoon like. Keep the embossing smooth and only the tips are strongly white.

Use the extra-small ball tool to emboss the stamen poking out the flowers, and don't forget to add the little white dots.

Once you have completed the flowers turn the vellum over and place it on a solid surface, then use an eraser to rub out all the white pencil lines from the front of the vellum.

Pattern 9. Cat and Mouse

Cat and Mouse Template.

Cat and Mouse

To complete this project you will need:

- Vellum
- White pencil
- Black fine liner
- Extra-small ball tool
- Small ball tool
- Large ball tool
- Extra-large ball tool
- White wax – optional
- Eraser

Tracing

Trace all the black lines of the template in to the centre of the vellum using the white pencil. Use the black fine liner to trace the cat's eyes, whisker spots and the mouse's eye. Colour the black areas of the tracing so that they are solidly black; as shown on the template. Do not trace the red lines; these are there to help you when you start embossing the fur. The red lines show fur length and direction. Remember though that the lines are just a guide and your cat will need much more fur than is indicated on the template otherwise it will look bald.

Embossing - All the embossing is completed on the SAME side as the tracing.

Use a piece of white wax – such as a tea light – to very lightly go over the surface of the vellum where you are going to be embossing. This will help the ball tools to glide smoothly over the vellum.

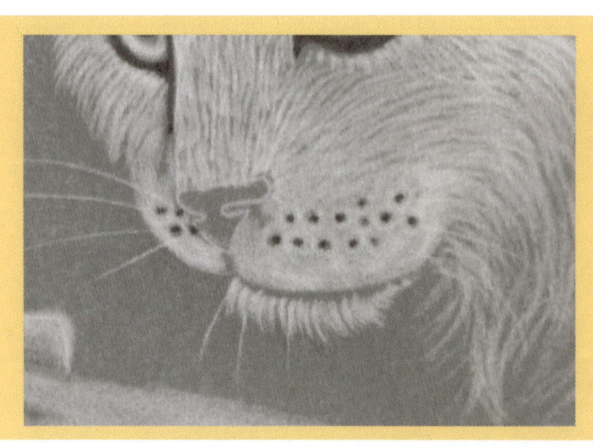

Cat Face

Use the large ball tool in small circles to emboss the cat's muzzle. The muzzle should be nice and smooth with as little variation in the depth of the white as possible. DO NOT emboss over the black whisker spots otherwise they will not show up when you turn the parchment over.

Leave the nose clear of embossing.

Starting above the nose begin embossing the cat's fur. Use the extra-small ball tool to create tiny flicks by pressing the ball into the vellum and gently flicking in the desired direction. The fur above the nose is very short and very regular but try not to go in rows when you emboss. Complete these tiny fur flicks up the face until you are roughly in line with the cat's eyes. From here the fur will start to get longer as it spreads over the top of the cat's head.

Use the extra-small ball tool to emboss the fur above the cat's muzzle.

All the Eyes

Start the cheek fur embossing from just *inside* the smooth embossing on the muzzle you completed earlier. This way the smooth embossing will gradually change to fur without a gap.

Use the extra-small ball tool to emboss a strong line of white over the top of the cat's eyes – this can be seen as a solid red line on the template. Be very careful not to go into the black outline of the eye. Use the small ball tool to emboss the tiny lines coming from beneath the cat's eyes.

The white lines over the tops of the eyes need to be blended into the rest of the embossing. Use the small ball tool to start embossing the fur on top of the cat's head, starting at the white lines you have just embossed, using the red lines on the template as a guide to fur length and direction. Once the top of the head is complete, follow the lines around the cheeks. Notice how the fur from the cheeks to back across the body is almost banded, with strong areas of fur and shadow. To create this, leave a gap in the embossing (an area with no embossing at all) after each line of fur.

Use the extra-small ball tool in a long single flick to add whiskers.

Cat Ears

Use the small ball tool to emboss the edges of the ears so that they are strongly white, (including the little flicks on the tips). Allow this to fade as the embossing moves around the edges of the ears towards the head.

Use the large ball tool to very lightly shade the inner ear – this embossing should be barely visible. When you emboss the cat's head make sure plenty of fur is covering the ear opening.

Cat Body

Using the small ball tool, emboss the fur on the cat's body using the template as a guide. The cat's body fur is much longer than that on the face but much simpler as it all follows the same curve. Build the fur up gradually; remember you can always add more embossing but you can't take any away.

IMPORTANT

Smoothing

So far all the embossing you have done on the body has been with the small ball tool. This is much too harsh for a cat's fur so you need to soften it with the large ball tool. Gently go over all the embossing, smoothing the lines until the cat looks nice and soft.

Cat Eyes

Use the extra-small ball tool to add the glint in the top right of the cat's pupils. This is a bit nerve-wrecking after all the hard work you have done so far as the pupil is coloured black and you won't be able to see what you are doing! But be brave and add a simple single line that follows the shape of the pupil edge. Keep turning the parchment over to check how you are doing.

Use the large ball tool to emboss the iris. The base of the iris is strongly white and this fades very quickly towards the top of the eye.

Cat Paw

Use the large ball tool to emboss the cat's paw just the same as you did the muzzle, working in small circles to create a smooth effect. Leave a gap in the embossing between the toes. Use the extra-large ball tool to continue this embossing up the leg until the fur starts again (shown by red lines on the template).

Use the small ball tool to emboss the cat's leg fur.

Mouse

The mouse is much scruffier than the cat and won't need any of the smoothing. Use the small ball tool to complete all the fur embossing. Emboss the mouse's chest and hind leg slightly whiter than the rest of the body.

Use the extra-small ball tool to emboss the edge of the ears strongly white. Use the extra-small ball tool to add the little glint in the mouse's eye, just the same as you did for the cat.

Use the extra-small ball tool to emboss over the lines on the top of the paws and tail. Don't emboss the lines where the paws are in contact with the table – you want these parts to look as if they are in shadow. Use the small ball tool to very lightly shade just behind these embossed lines. The tip of the mouse's tail should be strongly white.

Table

Use the extra-small ball tool to go over all the lines of the table so that they are strongly white.

Use the extra-large ball tool to lightly emboss the whole of the table so that the edges nearest the cat are more strongly white and this fades as it gets further away from the edge.

Pattern 10. Christmas Robins

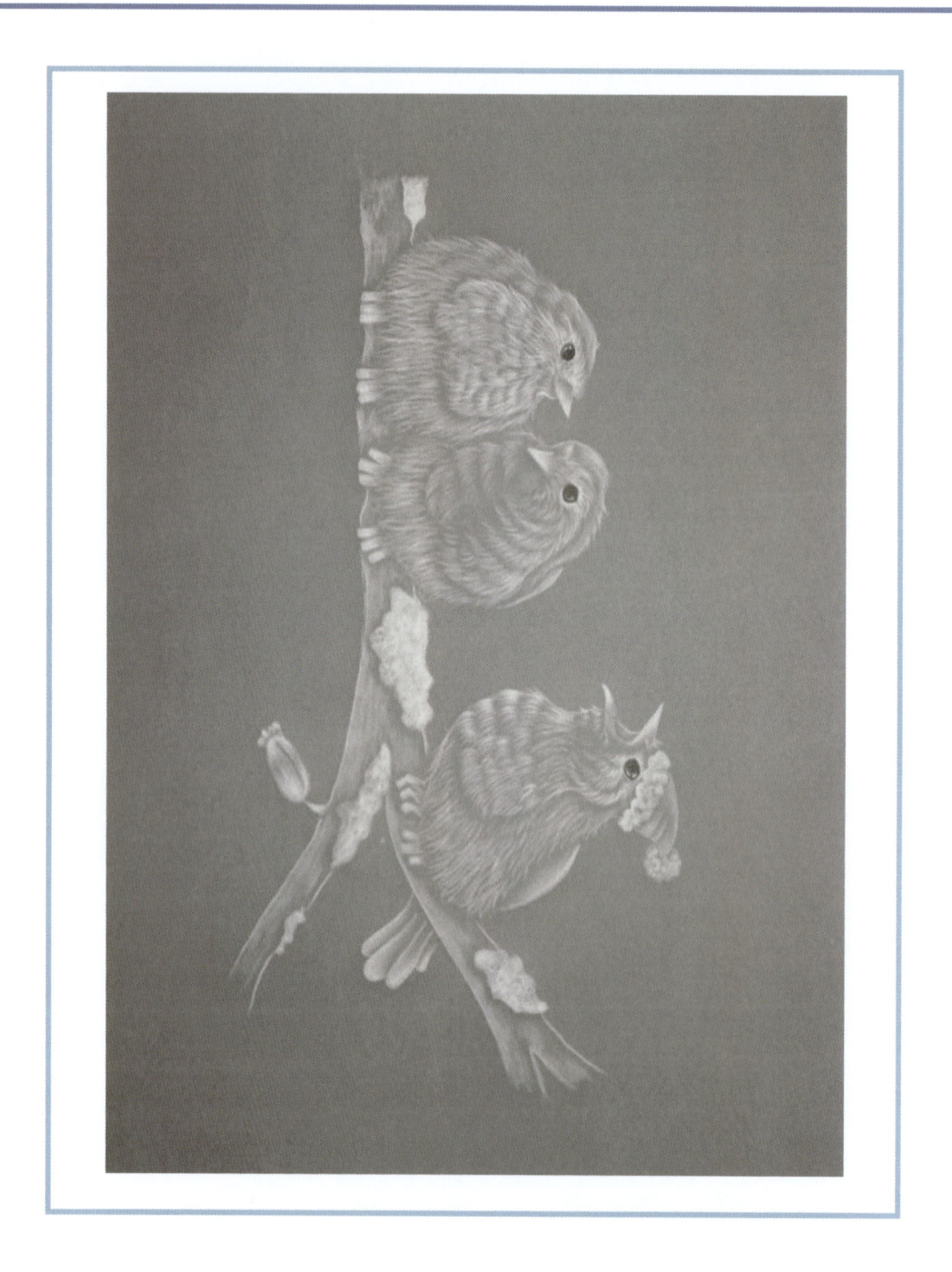

Robins Template

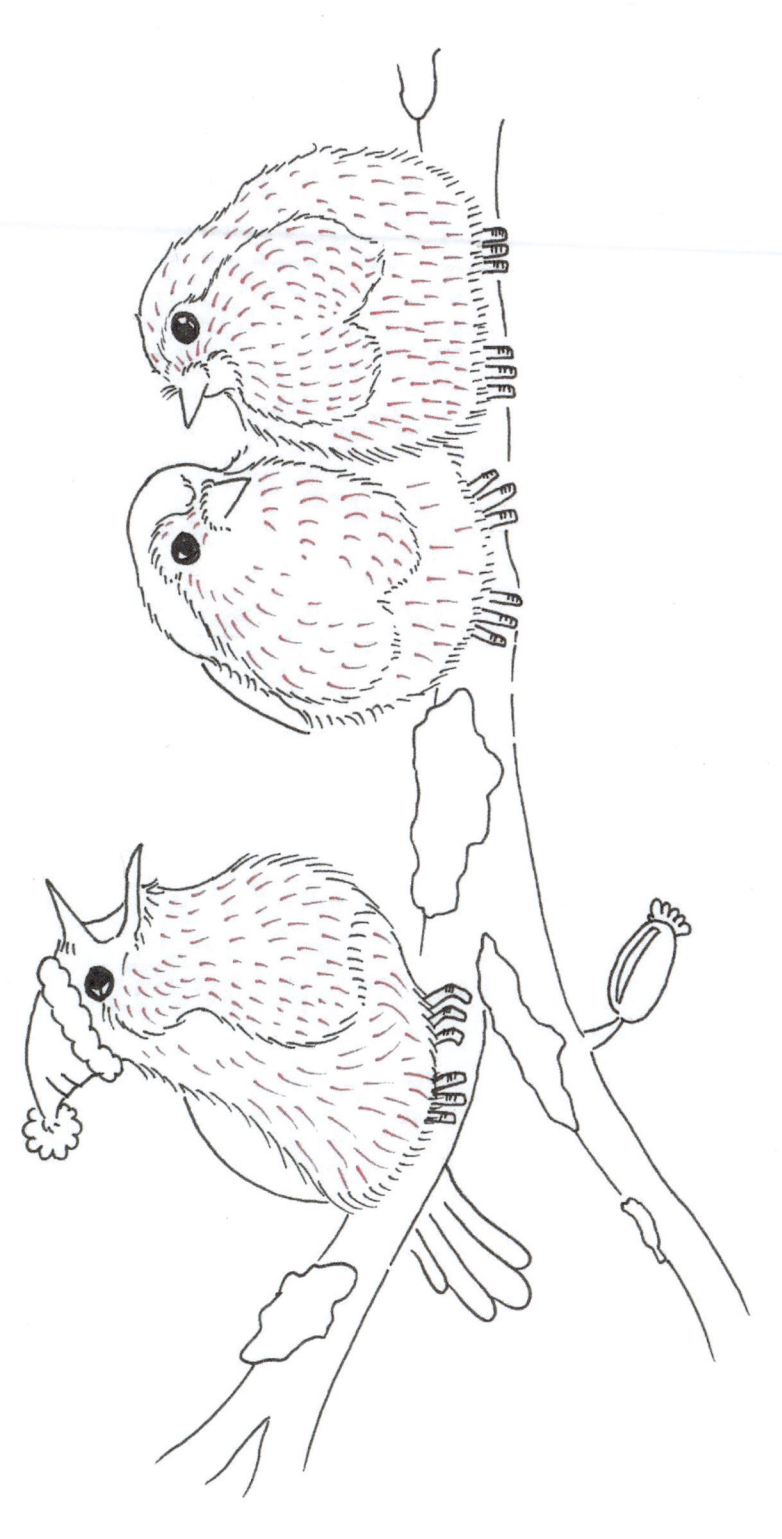

Christmas Robins

Tracing:

Trace all the black lines using the white pencil.

DO NOT trace the red lines. These are only there to help you emboss your robin's feathers.

Once the robins are traced, turn the parchment over. Colour the robin's eyes in with the black fine liner. All embossing is completed on the SAME side as the black fine liner.

All of the three robins are embossed in the same way – using the same tools for the same parts of the bird.

To complete this project you will need:

- Vellum and embossing mat
- White pencil
- Black fine liner
- Extra-small ball tool
- Small ball tool
- Large ball tool
- Extra-large ball tool

Embossing

Emboss the robin's eye first as this is the most important part of the whole picture. Use the extra-small ball-tool to emboss a soft line around each eye and then use the small ball tool to fade this back into the face.

Use the extra-small ball tool to add the tiny glints in the eye itself.

Use the small ball-tool to emboss the tip of the beak strongly white, then use the large ball-tool to fade the embossing back towards the face.

Feathers:

The red lines on the template show how the feathers are embossed including length and direction.

Use the small ball-tool to emboss all the feathers on the breast and face using the same simple flick motion that you use to create fur. Please note that you will need to do more flicks than are on the template otherwise the robins will look half bald!

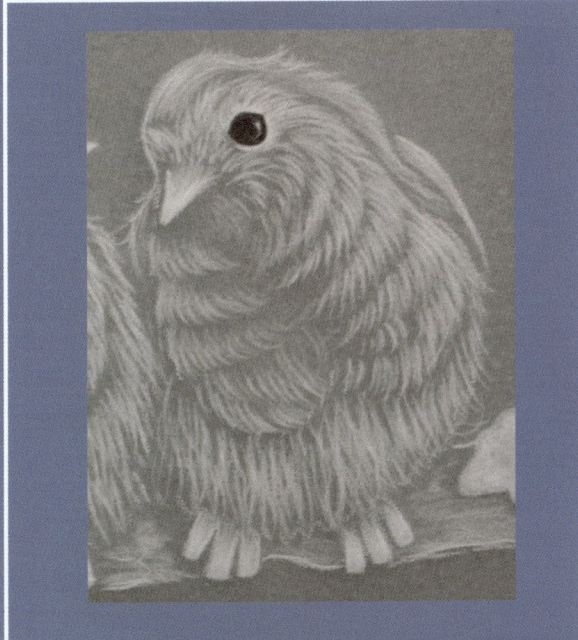

Breast

Usually I would always say to emboss feathers in tufts rather than rows - the robins are an exception. By embossing in rows you create a more rounded effect, making the birds look fatter.

Pay attention to where the robins are in shadow, such as underneath the chin and around the wings. These shadow area need far fewer feather flicks.

Also note how the feathers are shorter in the middle of the breast compared to the edges.

Body

The feathers on the lower half of the body are much longer and a bit more straggly than those on the breast. Complete these in the same way as the breast, only this time using a longer flick. Once you have done this use the large ball tool to gently go over the belly feathers, this will soften them and make the birds look a tad more cuddly.

Leave a gap in the embossing of roughly 1mm around the edge of the breast and face feathers.

Use the large ball tool to very lightly emboss the top of the head so that it is smooth and more strongly white on the outer edge.

Use the extra-small ball-tool to add a few little flicks coming off the robin's neck, sides and belly to make them look a bit scruffy.

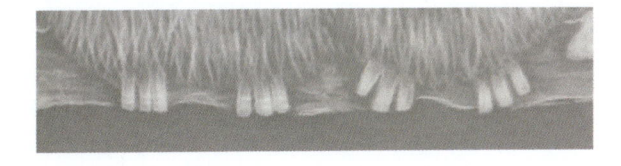

Feet

Use the small ball tool to emboss the toes so that they are white on the tips and fade towards the body.

Wings

Use the large ball tool to very lightly

emboss the wings visible on the right and middle robins. The wings need to be more strongly white on the outside and paler towards the body. Use the tool in long strokes from one end to the other to create as smooth an effect as possible.

Tail

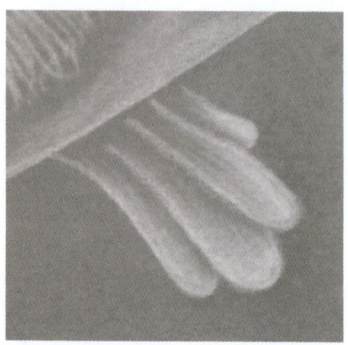

Use the extra-small ball tool to go over all the traced lines of the tail on the right hand robin. Use the small, then large, ball tools to emboss each feather individually so that the end is strongly white and this fades towards the body. Leave a very slight gap between the feathers so that they stand proud from each other.

Branch

Use the extra-large ball tool to very lightly emboss the branch so that it is evenly white all over with a gap of roughly 2mm around the robins and snow patches.

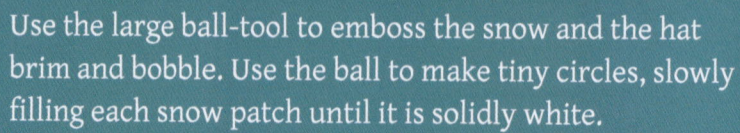

Snow

Use the large ball-tool to emboss the snow and the hat brim and bobble. Use the ball to make tiny circles, slowly filling each snow patch until it is solidly white.

Use the large ball tool to emboss the hat, leaving a shadow at the base of each fold and running up the centre from the brim to the bobble.

Berry

Use the small ball tool to emboss the berry so that both ends are strongly white. Leave the central strip clear of embossing. Use the extra-small ball-tool to emboss the tips of the leaflets on the end of the berry.

Tiny Templates

All the art in this book is intended just to be enjoyed as is, but I know there are times when you want to give your parchment as a gift.

Handmade cards are a great way to do this.

But.

Greetings cards are often something you want to be able to complete quickly, and you just don't have the time to devote hours to creating a card. This next section is a bonus. It's all the templates at half size – perfect for cards.

Tiny Template 2. Harvest Mice

Tiny Template 1. Eagles

Tiny Template 3. Howling Wolf					Tiny Template 4. Macaw

You will find with most of the templates that now they are smaller you need to reduce the size of ball tool that you use for each part. So if the original project said to use a large ball tool, then you may find the small ball is now more suitable with the tiny templates.

Experiment with your parchment craft, the more you do, the easier it will become to select the right tool for the right part of the pattern.

Tiny Template 5. Tiger Cub

Tiny Template 6. Rock Dragon

Tiny Template 7. Pegasus

Tiny Template 8. Hummingbird

Tiny Template 9. Cat and Mouse

Tiny Template 10. Christmas Robins.

NOTES

Make any notes you would like to remember about your parchment crafting here.

Parchment Craft
Embossing Art
Volume 1.

By Lauren Berry

For more information on patterns by Lauren Berry

Please visit the website at:

www.lozzberry.com

COMING SOON!

Parchment Craft Embossing Art Volume 2.

Printed in Great Britain
by Amazon